How
Candy Canes
Are Made

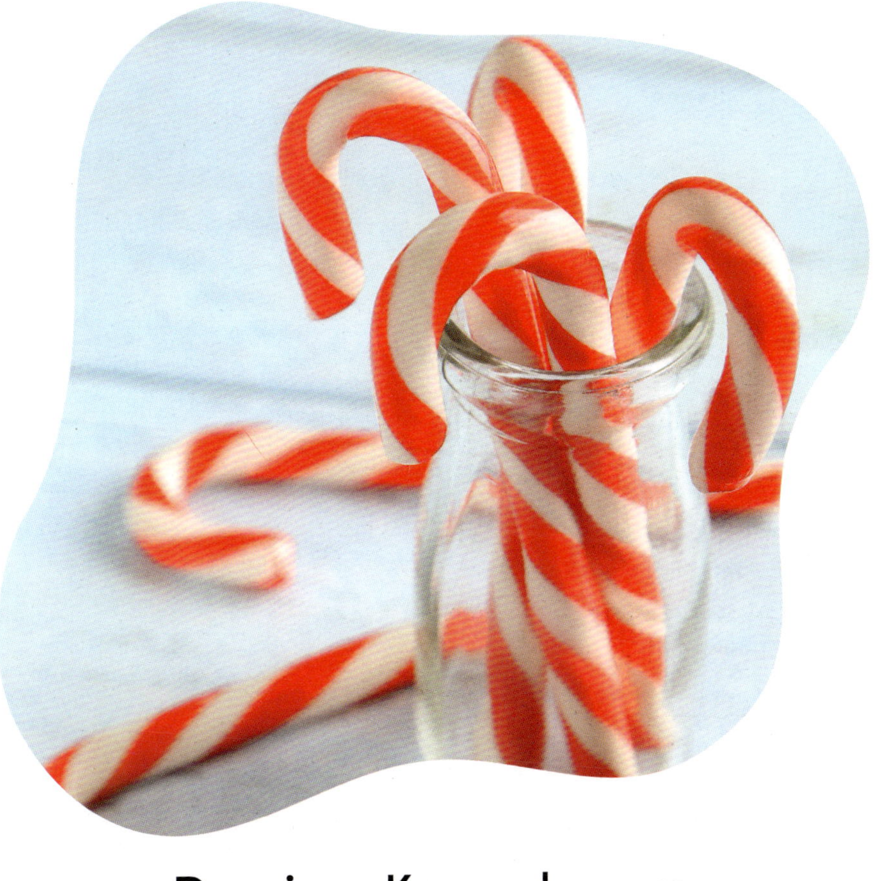

Danica Kassebaum

Consultant

Jamey Acosta, M.S.Ed.
Reading Specialist and English Learner TOSA

Publishing Credits

Rachelle Cracchiolo, M.S.Ed., *Publisher*
Emily R. Smith, M.A.Ed., *SVP of Content Development*
Véronique Bos, *VP of Creative*
Dona Herweck Rice, *Senior Content Manager*

Image Credits: all images from iStock and/or Shutterstock

Library of Congress Cataloging in Publication Control Number: 2024039314

5482 Argosy Avenue
Huntington Beach, CA 92649
www.tcmpub.com
ISBN 979-8-7659-9729-1
© 2025 Teacher Created Materials, Inc.
Printed by: 51497
Printed in: China

Table of Contents

What Are Candy Canes?

Candy canes are hard candies.

They have stripes and hooks. Most often, the stripes are red and white.

Many people buy candy canes at Christmas. But they can be sweet treats all year long.

Making Candy Canes

Candy canes are made with three main things. They are made of **sugar**, water, and **corn syrup**. The sugar has to get very hot. It gets so hot it melts.

melting sugar

cooling table

Next, the sugar must cool. The candy maker uses a special table. It is a cooling table. The table gets very cold to cool the candy mix.

Now, it is time to **stretch** the candy. A **machine** pulls the candy again and again.

Then, flavor is added to the candy. The candy maker can choose any flavor.

peppermint

Flavors

Candy canes come in all flavors. They can taste like fruit. Most taste like peppermint.

stretching machine

The next step is to warm the candy. Warming makes the candy soft. It gets soft enough to **mold**. Then, it is rolled into a large, heavy log.

At last, the candy is ready to become the candy cane we all know. It is time for stripes and a hook!

Stripes and Hooks

Strips of colored sugar are wrapped around the log. This will make the stripes of the candy canes.

The whole thing is pulled and stretched again. It becomes very long.

Red and White

The first candy canes were white. Now, they are mostly white with red stripes. But they can be made in any color.

The candy maker rolls the stretched candy. It looks like a long rope.

Now, it is ready to be cut. The pieces will become the candy canes. Pieces can also be cut into bite-sized candies.

The last step is to make the hooks. The top of each piece is bent. The bend is the hook.

No one knows for sure why a candy cane has a hook. It may be so that it looks like a **shepherd** staff.

shepherd staff

Sweet Treat

Some candy canes are made by hand.

Some candy canes are made with machines.

People love them no matter how they are made! They are always a sweet treat.

Let's Do Science

Have you ever wondered if the stripes on candy canes can come off? Experiment to find out!

What to Get

- 3 clear plastic cups
- 3 candy canes
- warm water
- cold water
- vinegar

What to Do

- Label your cups "vinegar," "cold water," and "warm water."

- Fill each cup with what is on the label.

- Place one candy cane in each cup.

- Watch to see what happens!

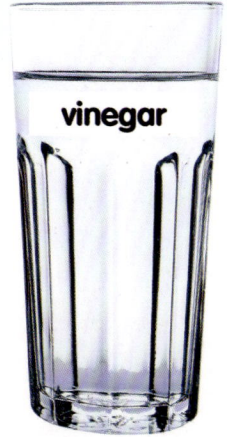

vinegar

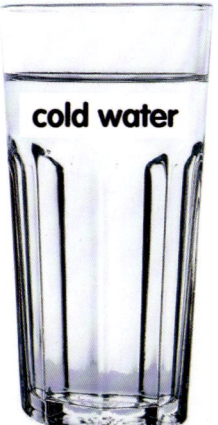

cold water

warm water

Glossary

corn syrup—a thick liquid made from cornstarch and sugar

machine—piece of equipment with moving parts that does work

mold—to form or press into a shape

shepherd—a person who takes care of sheep in a herd

stretch—to make something wider or longer by pulling it

sugar—a sweet powder or crystal that comes from plants